BRITAIN'S HERITAGE

Narrow Boats

Tom Chaplin

AMBERLEY

First published 2017

Amberley Publishing
The Hill, Stroud
Gloucestershire, GL5 4EP

www.amberley-books.com

Copyright © Tom Chaplin 2017

The right of Tom Chaplin to be identified as
the Author of this work has been asserted in
accordance with the Copyrights, Designs and
Patents Act 1988.

ISBN 978 1 4456 6997 7 (paperback)
ISBN 978 1 4456 6998 4 (ebook)

British Library Cataloguing in Publication Data.
A catalogue record for this book is available from
the British Library.

Printed in the UK.

Contents

1
Introduction

Today, the term 'narrow boat' tends to conjure up images of a purpose-built, steel-hulled pleasure cruiser, whereas before 1970 it referred to a cargo-carrying boat on the narrow canal system, often with a family living aboard. The modern, leisure 'narrowboat', as they have come to be known, only emerged gradually in the mid-1960s. Back then, if you went on a boat holiday you would almost certainly have headed for either the Broads or the Thames.

The narrow boat was conceived at a meeting at The George Hotel in Lichfield in 1769, when the proprietors of the various narrow canals that were just starting to be built met to agree the optimum dimensions. A consensus was reached at approximately 70 ft long by 7 ft wide. Initially there were two types of boat – one long-distance with living accommodation, built of wood and towed by a horse; the other short-haul, on which the rudder could be hung at either end to save turning. These sometimes had a small cabin to provide shelter or modest facilities for a night's sleep – probably the equivalent of a modern lorry sleeper cab.

Above: This print appeared at the time of the Regent's Park explosion in 1874 and indicates that commercial narrow boats remained much the same until the end of trading. (Tom Chaplin)
Left: A group of Joey boats in Birmingham. (Tom Chaplin)

They were normally built alongside the canal and launched sideways into the water. Sometimes, itinerant journeymen boatbuilders rented a patch of canal-side land, but there were also more substantial establishments that built under cover, usually a corrugated roof with a large span. The basic construction was a flat elm bottom with oak planks curved by heating them in a steam chest, often fired by wood from boats that had been broken up. They frequently had second-hand iron knees. The stem post was usually a hand-picked oak branch with a suitable curve, which was then refined with an adze. A blacksmith provided hand-made nails, along with the iron stem bar and steel

An advertisement for Samuel Barlow, showing the launching of *Hazel* in 1957 at its Braunston yard. (Tom Chaplin)

Wooden boats were built of oak planks cut by saw and shaped where necessary with an adze, as shown here. (Tom Chaplin)

Ex-FMC *Chiltern* being fitted with new planks at Charity Dock in 1967. (Tom Chaplin)

The graceful bow of Barlow's *Hazel* after a repaint in 1963. (Tom Chaplin)

Mass-produced narrow boats at Yarwood's Dock, in Northwich, on the Weaver. (Hugh McKnight Photography)

sheeting to protect the boat when travelling through ice. The finished hull was caulked and painted with chalico – a mixture of tar, horse hair and dung!

Iron and steel boats were only made in a few places that had the equipment to shape the plates, lift them and produce rivets; these form the majority of the surviving craft. There were very few docks for steel boats. Harland & Wolff, creators of the *Titanic*, built narrow boats exclusively for the Grand Union Canal Carrying Company (GUCCCo) at their Woolwich yard. They are often referred to as Woolwiches. The majority of craft were built for a wide range of companies by Yarwoods of Northwich and they were known as Northwiches.

Not all tunnels were built with towpaths and, before the advent of tugs, the horse would be led above ground to the other end while the rest of the crew 'legged' the boat through. This entailed lying on planks cantilevered out on each side of the bow, and, keeping a firm grip, walking along the tunnel sides, hauling the boat as they did so.

In time, horses gave way to steam tugs, later to steam narrow boats and, eventually, to diesel engines. The boats themselves have not always been spoken of as narrow boats. In London and the Thames, they were often called 'Monkey boats' after the son of a Severn barge-builder, Thomas Monk of Lower Mitton, now the town of Stourport. Born in 1765, Thomas Junior is said to have designed the living cabin on horse-drawn craft when he was a young Black Country entrepreneur. Since he ultimately owned a fleet of 133, each of which would have had his name emblazoned on the side (in compliance with the canal regulations), it is hardly surprising that the name stuck. On the Severn they were often termed 'long boats', while day boats in Birmingham were usually known as 'Joey boats' after Joe Worsey, who was the the most prolific builder of such boats in the Birmingham area.

A pair of leggers about to enter Maida Vale Tunnel. (Hugh McKnight Photography)

Above: Further along the canal, a black-and-white-liveried FMC pair wait for the tunnel tug at Islington. The steam from the tug can be seen behind the boats. (Hugh McKnight Photography)

Below: The motor has a rounded stern, a counter and a tubular steel tiller. The cabin is longer to accommodate the engine, which is accessed through side doors and a gunwale. In contrast, the butty has a raised stern and a cockpit but no gunwales. Both the large rudder and the tiller are wooden and the boat greatly resembles its precursor, the horse-drawn narrow boat. (Tom Chaplin)

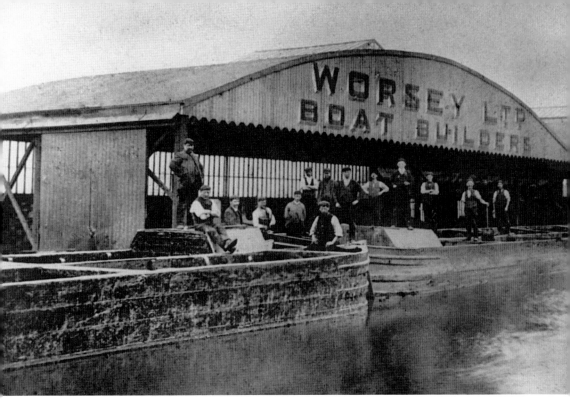

Joe Worsey's dock on the BCN. (Hugh McKnight Photography)

The canals and hence the narrow boat were a major catalyst in the Industrial Revolution and consequently helped to define the England that we have today. One horse could tow a boat with 100 times more cargo than could be loaded onto a pack horse and about twenty-five times more than a horse and cart. This enabled the first step in a major transport revolution. Before the canals, the only cities that could expand were those on navigable rivers because it was too expensive to bring food and fuel in and to take goods and waste out. The cycle of improvements is well illustrated by the Shropshire Union Canals (SU), especially on what is now called the Llangollen but was originally the Ellesmere Canal. That part of Shropshire had the right climate for dairying but there was no point in exceeding local needs while a wider market was inaccessible.

This changed when the canal was linked to limestone quarries where the lime was used as a fertiliser on the adjoining land, producing rich grass and a greatly increased milk yield. The excess milk was turned into cheese, which was delivered by boat into the centre of Manchester. The people of Ellesmere promoted the canal, but while their town has grown very little in the last 200 years, the small hamlet on the banks of the tidal Mersey where the waterway terminated is now the large conurbation of Ellesmere Port.

Birmingham and the Black Country grew up around the canal network. The population of Birmingham was only 42,250 in 1778, yet by 1931 it was in excess of a million. The canals meant that the area's abundant resources of coal, limestone and iron could readily be brought in to supply the burgeoning industries that relied on them. Elsewhere, people like Josiah Wedgwood, who sponsored the Trent & Mersey Canal, benefitted from the low cost of importing the raw material and of exporting the finished product, as well as a significant reduction in breakages.

Canal-building continued into the railway era and many canals reached their peak tonnage during the Edwardian period. After the First World War, a number of factors led to a steady

The restored Shropshire Union horse boat *Saturn*, built for carrying cheese from Cheshire to Manchester. Because of her sleek lines, she was only capable of carrying 18 tons rather than the usual 25. (Tom Chaplin)

decline and by then over half the canals were owned by railway companies. In a few cases this was an advantage but others suffered under a monopoly. With the 1947 Transport Act, the Labour Government nationalised the railways and found itself forced to take over the majority of the canals. This included all those that were railway-owned and those that had been run by the government during the Second World War. During this period, the building of motorways became the biggest threat and the nationalised fleet of narrow boats was privatised in 1963 and 1964. The last regular, long-distance traffic ceased in 1970.

Did you know?

At one time, virtually everything was carried by boat, whether it was soldiers; ice for Boots, the chemist; considerable consignments of raw materials; dangerous goods such as gunpowder and benzoline, or nearly all the tea that was drunk in Birmingham.

The demise of the family narrow boat changed the culture of the canals. Speed and working efficiency were no longer of the essence so skills declined, the painting of the boats began to lose touch with tradition, and art on the new craft became much more diverse. This book offers an introductory account of how 200 years of carrying brought about the organic development of efficient craft and examines how they were run, how they were decorated, and what life aboard was like.

Looking back now, it seems incredible that a whole family could have lived in a space just 8 ft 9 inches long and 6 ft 6 inches wide. Yet, at the time of the early Industrial Revolution, the colourful boatman's cabin may well have seemed preferable to overcrowded back-to-back slums-dark rooms often only 12 ft square and with poor sanitation, overlooking narrow streets blackened by the outpourings of factory chimneys. In those days, the lack of numeracy and literacy seemed acceptable, but after the Second World War the need to educate children who could no longer rely on a future career in carrying drove many boatpeople to move to the land.

Right: A tug tows two cabinless Joeys through the BCN main line with a blast furnace in the background. (Tom Chaplin) **Below**: A BW ex-FMC motor loaded with coal tied up at a wharf in the Potteries – a scene utterly lost now that most of the industry has gone. (Tom Chaplin)

Pictured here on a Monday morning with two pairs of boats is the famous jam works with its private basin off the Paddington Arm. The butty *Lucy* has been emptied and the process continues aboard *Ian*. By the following evening, this pair would have reached Braunston Top Lock, 86 miles and eighty-three locks further north. The barrels of fruit pulp on the right would have arrived by barge from London's docks. (Tom Chaplin)

Since then, prohibitively expensive housing or a wish for an alternative lifestyle has meant that narrow boats have again become homes to many. The canals are so awash with leisure craft that temporary moorings in many key sites are hard to find. Yet to those of us who still remember the surge of excitement created by the sound of a distant Bolinder announcing the approach of a commercial narrow boat – that exquisitely painted emblem of a disappearing age – something irreplaceable has been lost.

A perfect pair of Barlow's boats makes haste as water builds up around their bows. (Tom Chaplin)

2
Brief History

Not a lot is known about the very early wooden horse-drawn narrow boats but they probably resembled the craft that up to then had been used on the river. It has never been firmly ascertained whether the original cabins were laid out in the way now commonly accepted as traditional, or even whether they were decorated. Some early engravings feature boats that greatly resemble the narrow boat as we know it but we cannot be entirely sure that they offer a faithful representation.

Riveted iron boats built in the latter part of the nineteenth century have had a remarkably long life. For example, *Australia*, built in 1894, is still in working trim. The very last wooden boat to be built was the *Raymond*, launched in 1958, now based at Braunston and preserved by the Friends of *Raymond*. By the 1870s, steam haulage had become common for towing boats through tunnels as well as on long, lock-free sections such as the Ashby Canal and Birmingham.

By Act of Parliament, canal companies were initially forbidden to run their own carrying operations. During this period, one of the largest fleets was that of the well-known firm of Pickford. Its business incorporated delivery and collection vehicles, warehouses and narrow boats. By 1838, it not only had 116 narrow boats but over 1,000 horses. When the Regents Canal was opened in 1820, Pickford transferred its London headquarters from Paddington on the Grand Union Canal (GU) to the new City Road Basin. Horse-drawn vehicles collected from all over the metropolis during the day and the boats set off in the evening with goods destined for the far-flung corners of England.

This engraving, first published in 1873, shows a typical horse boat replete with the familiar form of decoration that changed little during the next century. (Tom Chaplin)

Above: *Roger* and *Raymond* are held up by a lock stoppage at Rickmansworth while Mrs Bray smiles at the camera. (Tom Chaplin)
Below: Pickford's headquarters in City Road Basin on the Regents Canal in 1827. (Tom Chaplin)

In 1839, the notorious murder of Christina Collins by boatmen aboard a Pickford boat on the Trent & Mersey Canal dealt a bitter blow to the reputation of canal passenger-carrying. It was widely acknowledged that many captains had perfected the technique of extracting spirits from the carboys on board in a way that defied detection and on this occasion it had devastating results. Several witnesses testified to having seen the terrified woman seeking to escape the attentions of a drunk and abusive crew. Her body was later found floating in the canal. Pickford did have a trial of some steam boats in 1842, but at about this time it moved across to the railways.

The Canal Carriers Act of 1845 gave canal companies the right to act as carriers and, as a result, the Grand Junction Canal Company (today the Southern Grand Union) started a carrying department and introduced steam-powered narrow boats that over the succeeding years attracted some unwelcome publicity.

Did you know?

Blisworth tunnel is 3,056 yards long (1.75 miles) and has no towpath so steam tugs were a welcome development. By 1914, the first tug of the day left the south end at 5 a.m. and then ran every two hours until 7 p.m. The tug returned from the north portal at 6 a.m. and operated two hourly until 8 p.m. During the winter the first and last journeys were omitted.

In 1861, unforeseen hazards resulted in fatalities aboard the *Bee* as it navigated Blisworth tunnel. The resulting inquest offered some insight into the running of such boats. *Bee* ran scheduled trips between London and Birmingham. The engine was always cleaned in London and examined by an engineer in Birmingham. On this occasion, after leaving Buckby, the crew realised that the engine was not working efficiently so they stopped at Blisworth, cleaned out the clinker, and stoked up the fire. They then waited at the tunnel entrance until there was enough steam to take them through as they wanted to avoid adding any more fuel once inside. By all accounts, the wind entering the tunnel was travelling at roughly the same speed as the boat, so the toxic fumes built up around the craft. By the time they came out, two men had died of asphyxiation and another two had collapsed and sustained burns as they landed close to the boiler. After this, extra airshafts were opened up in both Blisworth and Braunston tunnels to help to minimise pollution.

Then, on 2 October 1874, a spark from a steam tug towing three pairs of narrow boats through Regent's Park ignited petroleum and gunpowder for blasting carried aboard the *Tilbury*, causing an explosion as it passed under Macclesfield Bridge. Bridge and boat were both destroyed, the crew were all killed and one of the other boats was sunk. Nearby properties were badly damaged and so significant was the shock felt up to 12 miles away that an earthquake was suspected. When it was rebuilt, the cast-iron Coalbrookdale columns that had supported it were re-used and it became known as Blow Up Bridge.

As a result of these incidents, the Grand Junction gave up its carrying fleet. Various small companies were started, and over a period of time, with mergers and acquisitions, they were taken over by Fellows Morton & Clayton Ltd (FMC), which became the largest narrow boat operator. It certainly had the largest fleet of steam boats, which worked from London to Birmingham and Nottingham. Many of the hulls of their iron steamers are still on the canal network and one in particular, the *President*, has been fully restored to steam.

Above: A steam tug emerges from Blisworth tunnel with a train of narrow boats behind. (Hugh McKnight Photography)

Left: The cast columns of Macclesfield Bridge on the Regents Canal can be seen protruding from the rubble. Today the reconstructed bridge is known as Blow Up Bridge. (Tom Chaplin)

Steam narrow boats never became very popular, partly because the additional crew that they required for 24-hour working, as well as the space taken up by the boiler and engine, greatly reduced carrying capacity. To compensate for this, they began to tow what would otherwise have been a horse-drawn boat – a butty. FMC's steamer fleet bore a variety of titles that reflected their power, with names like *Sultan* and *Princess*. They provided a fast service that worked to a timetable, usually with a young male crew who hot-bedded. The coming of the diesel engine in 1911 replaced the steamers and by 1927 they were no longer to be seen. Most boats worked in pairs: a motor and a butty on which families lived permanently afloat, no longer labouring around the clock, but nevertheless still working an extended day.

Although narrow boats were commonly 72 ft by 7 ft, typically with a capacity of 25 tons and draught of 4 ft 6 inches, there were significant variations brought about by the requirements of both the waterway on which they operated and the nature of the cargo carried. Companies soon learned to exploit the fact that most locks were built slightly oversize and craft of 7 ft 1 inch became common. On the Wolverhampton level, 'Ampton boats, towed by tugs, worked the long, lock-free section from the Cannock coalfields and were 86 ft by 7 ft 9 inches, which increased their carrying capacity by 36 per cent. At the other end of the scale, when the Newport branch of the Shropshire Union Canal (SU) connected up with the Shrewsbury

The FMC steamer *Phoenix* at Buckby. Note the large funnel and long cabin. The person in the centre is the toll officer. By measuring the dry side and using Archimedes' principle, he would calculate the tonnage with the aid of gauging tables. (Hugh McKnight Photography)

Above: The butty *Raymond* – the last working wooden narrowboat to be built. Constructed in 1958 by Samuel Barlow Coal Co. Ltd, she was designed for the carriage of coal. The coal is piled up well above the gunwale level with wooden 'slack' boards so that it can be stacked against the cabin. The boat is fine-lined to ensure a quick trip when it returned empty to the collieries. (Tom Chaplin)

Below: The large Northwich-built *Renfrew* approaches the three locks at Soulbury towing *Lucy*. On *Renfrew*, the coal is all below gunwale level because she was built with a variety of cargos in mind and, with top cloths, would have been suitable for grain. In contrast, *Lucy* is well down in the water with coal stacked high. Despite appearances, both the boats have the same draught. (Tom Chaplin)

Canal, which had been built for trains of narrow tub boats, craft were built with a much-reduced width of 6 ft 2 inches, while the entrepreneurs carrying salt from Middlewich to Anderton made use of canal subsidence from salt mining and built extra deep craft.

Ex-working boats often appear to differ considerably in shape and this is usually related to their original function. On the Samuel Barlow Coal Company's large fleet of craft, the boatmen often unloaded coal with a shovel, so to make this easier the hull sides were kept as low as possible, since coal could be stacked above gunwale level. To enable the emptied boats to travel fast on the return trip, they had a sleek hull shape. On the other hand, the GU craft had higher sides because one of their staple traffics was grain, which could not be heaped up and had to be kept dry.

One of the most revered types of boat, known as 'Joshers' (after Joshua Fellows), belonged to FMC. This nineteenth-century hull design in iron has lasted well into the twenty-first century. Their traffics were, in the main, containerised, not the familiar ones of today but sacks, tea chests, crates for bottled goods like vinegar, wooden or cardboard cases for tinned goods, and since the ability to carry the maximum volume was more important than the tonnage, they tended to have high running planks and cloths. FMC also had specialist boats such as those designed to carry tubes from Stewarts and Lloyds, on which the hold was recessed into the motor cabin to create additional stowage length. Associated Canal Carriers, which became the Grand Union Company, built their Royalty Class boats with high sides and bluff bows because they travelled down the tidal Thames. Narrow boats on the River Severn also had higher sides but with large wooden towing posts so that a string of boats, normally horse-drawn on the canal, could be towed behind a tug.

There appeared to be no consensus among working boatmen about which might be considered the best boat. Their accounts were usually highly subjective and more than anything else, reflected their loyalty and affection for a particular craft and probably the cargoes and routes they were using. Some prioritised speed rather than tonnage, others prioritised greater headroom and a bigger cabin. A few favoured the rather ugly, but high-capacity Runcorn boats that were mechanically unloaded when they reached the gasworks. Their bluff, ungainly hull-shape was of no consequence on the wide, deep, lock-free Bridgewater Canal. On the other

FMC steamers often transferred their load into a horse boat at Braunston as the canal was still narrow from there to Birmingham. The cargo comprises Lyle's Syrup and Worcestershire Sauce. (Hugh McKnight Photography)

This picture shows two motors, both built at Yarwood's yard at Northwich in the 1930s. The large motor, *Linda*, on the right, was built as the Royalty Class *Victoria* and was designed so that she could be used on the tideway. *Cypress*, built for FMC, was intended for cased goods. (Tom Chaplin)

hand, the handleability of FMC's Braithwaite fine-lined butties secured their popularity as part of a pair negotiating the double locks from the Cheshire Plain up the Trent & Mersey. They did not reach their full beam until as far back as the mast so the butties could swivel in and reach the cill. Bluff boats had to be pulled the last couple of feet by hand.

The SU emerged as a result of the amalgamation of a group of canals and the formation of the Shropshire Union Railway & Canal Company (SUR&CC). It intended to convert canals to railways and to expand the railway system elsewhere. In the event, no canals were converted but were instead leased to the London & North-Western Railway (LNWR). It ceased to extend the rail track and created an integrated transport system, forming a monopoly through which it could infiltrate into other railways' territory. As an alternative to having boats that carried a nominal 25 tons, most of its fleet were fast fly boats with an 18-ton capacity, calling at warehouses en route to drop off and pick up goods. All were wooden and horse-drawn. Although it was not the sole carrier on its canal, it was by far the largest.

After the First World War, various railway companies merged and the SU came under the London, Midland & Scottish Railway (LMS), which in 1921 closed down its carrying department. Many of the traffics were taken on by other carriers. One well-known character, Charlie 'Chocolate' Atkins, was born aboard the SU horse boat *Rebecca* in 1902 and grew up to work for the company himself. However, these were uncertain times and to survive you had to be flexible. In 1921, when the SU ceased carrying, he worked for the newly formed Midland & Coast Carrying Company, which had been set up to take on many of the SU traffics. Eventually this company was swallowed up by FMC, which in turn was nationalised in 1949 and became part of British Waterways (BW).

Above: The motor on the inside was shaped like a motorised butty. These deep-sided Runcorn boats were not very attractive; however, they carried a high tonnage and were easy to work on the wide, long, lock-free Bridgewater Canal. (Tom Chaplin)

Below: The elegant lines of a Shropshire Union horse boat. The hull only reaches maximum width for a few feet of its length. The boat's name is carved into the top plank. (Hugh McKnight Photography)

In 1970, Charlie Atkins steers *Mendip* towards Preston Brook with a load of marble chips. Charlie took over *Mendip* when she was a year old in 1951 and stayed aboard, despite changing ownership, until shortly before he died in 1981. (Tom Chaplin)

In 1951, Charlie took over *Mendip*, one of the last Joshers to be built and which was only finished after nationalisation. For thirteen years, he worked on the Knighton to Bournville contract carrying chocolate mass, a feat that earned him his 'Chocolate' sobriquet. BW's northern fleet was privatised to become Willow Wren Canal Transport Services and a few years later the fleet changed hands again and became Anderton Canal Carrying Company. Charlie stayed with *Mendip* throughout. He was past retirement age when The Boat Museum at Ellesmere Port opened in the early 1970s and, unwilling to move to the land, he and *Mendip* became prime exhibits until close to his death in 1981.

In the London area, barges replaced the horse with diesel tractors but this never really applied to narrow boats. Moving a boat with a horse can be very efficient, especially in heavily locked sections. A well-trained horse knows when to stop and start and is actually a help at the locks. They therefore remained viable in Birmingham up to the end of carrying. Unpowered boats were moored outside factories where they acted as floating skips. When full, they would be towed away by horse. Nevertheless, there were a number of downsides to horses. They didn't have a union, but they certainly knew when they had had enough for the day and getting the horse ready in the morning, feeding him and bedding him down at night was a time-consuming affair. It was not a great economic bargain either because he still needed to be fed on days when you were waiting for orders. If he became ill, even with a good vet it could take a considerable time before he was back in action. Large companies would bring in other horses but the impact on an owner boatman or small company could be devastating. At times, a bad epidemic of equine flu could affect the whole industry. Most boatmen talked very fondly of their horses but accepted that in the end they had been superseded and could not withstand the financial and practical benefits of running a motorised boat.

Did you know?

The Pontcysyllte Aqueduct in North Wales carries the Llangollen Canal over the River Dee. It is 336 yards (307 m) long, 126 ft (38 m) high and only 4 yards (3.4 m) wide including the narrow towpath. Many boat horses refused to cross, especially on windy days. Then the boatman had to haul the boat across by himself while either his children or his wife walked the horse down, across the river and then back up the other side of the steep valley.

Above: For many years the horse was the most important means of propulsion. (Tom Chaplin)
Right: The horse tows away a Joey boat with a load of rubbish into Farmer's Bridge Top Lock. Note the simple towing mast and crude shape of the boat. (Tom Chaplin)

One of the difficulties of horse boating was crossing the Trent between the River Soar, the Erewash Canal and the Cranfleet Cut to Nottingham. Here a horse is being ferried across the river. (Tom Chaplin)

Initially, motor boats were powered by single-cylinder Bolinder diesel engines, of which every juddering stroke could be heard and, aboard, could be felt too, being visible in the concentric rings vibrating in a mug of tea. It must have been a tiring work environment. The other difficulty for anyone accustomed to handling horses was getting to grips with the engine. To get it started, it had to be heated with a blow lamp before you kicked the flywheel round to get it to fire. It was essential that you never let it cool down too much at tick-over in case it stalled. There was no gearbox. The trickiest bit of all on the early engines was putting the boat into astern. You had to slow the engine down before pulling a lever to cause the engine to backfire. Many older boatmen used to treat their motorboats more like horse boats, stopping them in locks with ropes rather than going astern. On one occasion a Number One (the name given to owner boatmen) took his horse boat to Bushell Brothers on the Wendover Arm and had it converted to diesel. He was given instructions on how to reverse the engine and he set off up the arm but when he got to the junction of the main line at Marsworth a short distance away, the boatyard heard a loud bang and some swearing and soon afterwards he reappeared on foot, towing his boat which had acquired a damaged bow. He had obviously revved up without the engine backfiring properly to put the boat astern.

In the 1930s, the Grand Union Company built up a large fleet of new narrow boats. These were mostly powered by what were then termed high-speed engines, supplied by Russell Newbery or by National JP engines, standing for joint production. These have now become the classic narrow boat engine.

A successful but now defunct craft was the swift, Scotch or packet boat. These fine, light craft were designed to be pulled by two galloping horses at between 10 and 12 miles an hour. They became very popular and an excellent way for people to move considerable distances at a much cheaper rate than a horse and carriage. One of the last indications is Paddington Packet Boat Dock near Uxbridge, which was the terminus from Paddington. There is also a pub nearby of the same name. Legend has it that the principle was discovered on the Paisley Canal (hence 'Scotch' boats) when a boatman was finishing for the day. A dog appeared, frightening his horse so that it bolted. The boatman thought that in no time at all the horse would tire but instead found himself travelling at over 10 miles an hour while producing virtually no wash.

A modern narrow beam workboat is on the inside while on the outside is an ex-ice breaker, originally horse-drawn when she was built in 1924, but motorised in 1942. (Hugh McKnight Photography)

This seemed too good to be true but over the next few weeks, trials showed that provided that the horse reached the optimum speed quickly, it could then be maintained with very little power. It was, in fact, riding on the soliton, or self-reinforcing solitary wave that it had created.

Technically under the term narrow boat are the ancillary craft, such as dredgers, icebreakers, bricklayers' flats, etc. All of these played an important role not only in maintaining and dredging the waterways but also in keeping the channel open in all but the most severe of winters. A loaded narrow boat will loosen the silt with each passage and plough a channel down the canal. There are historical precedents that demonstrate this sometimes dramatic effect.

In 1965, after the closure of Pooley Hall Colliery near Polesworth, Willow Wren Canal Transport Services Ltd found alternative loading for its Croxley traffic at the end of the Ashby Canal at Measham. The Ashby Canal had not been used since the Longford Power Station contract was lost in 1957 and, expecting the track to have silted up in the intervening period, on 24 May the first pair loaded only 42 tons to reduce the draught. In spite of this precaution, however, it took three days to complete the 22 miles. Nevertheless, the crew's dogged determination enabled them to begin to re-establish a channel and by the end of July the tonnage had increased to 48 tons 7 hundredweight. After six months, 50-ton loads were being carried and the boats were completing the trip in a day. This freight traffic effectively re-opened the canal and pleasure boats were the beneficiaries.

Did you know?

In 1859, colliery owners trading on the 30-mile lock-free Ashby Canal were banned from using steam tugs by the Midland Railway, which owned the canal, ostensibly because the wash from the propellers would damage the canal banks. A test case was taken to Chancery where the Master of the Rolls directed that experiments should take place to determine at what speed a tug would produce an injurious wave – in this case 3.5 mph. This was the start of speed limits on the canal. GU narrow boats often travelled at 5.5 mph empty but the official limit was 6 mph. Horse boats travelled at 2 mph loaded and 3 mph empty. At nationalisation, similar canals had different speed limits, those that had been railway owned being lower. Today's 4 mph is arbitrary.

3
Life Aboard

On the face of it, a cabin interior 8 ft 9 inches long, 6 ft 6 inches wide with barely standing headroom and the prospect of rising damp from the bilges would exemplify the most deprived living conditions in the country. Yet despite this and their lack of education, the overall impression was of a happy, contented floating community aboard what were often immaculate craft with polished brass, scrubbed rope-work and clean clothes. How was it done?

The boating population had much in common with pre-industrial society, centred as it was round a family enterprise, each member with his own designated task. Undoubtedly wages were poor: most were paid a flat rate per ton for a particular trip. The skill of the boatman, therefore, was to load on one hand as much as possible, but on the other, to avoid overloading because that would slow the craft down. They sometimes worked bizarre hours, starting off at 4 a.m. so that they could reach their destination in time to unload on a Friday afternoon. They could then work over the weekend and gain a considerable boost to their income.

Did you know?

Only the captain or skipper was paid for each journey so neither his wife nor his children was covered by insurance. Some companies refused to employ female captains. On a few occasions, a teenage son officially became captain when his father died, so that his widowed mother and siblings could carry on as before. If a childless couple employed a third hand, it was the captain's responsibility to pay him.

The exploitative rates of pay were to some extent offset by the low cost of living: no rent, no rates, no charge for filling up with water. In the days when central heating was rare, even the wealthy tended to huddle round a fire in draughty rooms before creeping along chilly passages to icy bedrooms. On the boats, enough coal was carried that heating was not a problem and families could indulge in the luxury of a fire in the bedroom every night. Many boatmen had lock-keeper friends or relatives keen to feed their chickens on the grain residue swept from the bilge and to hand out eggs in exchange. A bag of coal could be swapped for a sack of potatoes with a farmer.

Did you know?

Many boatmen had dogs, some of which were enthusiastic poachers on land adjoining the canal. A few were even trained to fetch duck eggs from nests. Pheasants, rabbits and hares were popular on the Northern Oxford before the canal was straightened. The boatman could cut across the fields, catch a rabbit and re-join his boat at the next bridge before it had finished its circuitous journey.

The boatmen could survive quite well and some were quick to seize any business opportunity that offered itself. On hearing the manager complaining about the cost of hay for the pit ponies, one owner-boatman bought some hay 60 miles away and made a good profit selling it to the colliery.

It is difficult today for people to appreciate just how fast and efficiently the skilled boatpeople worked their boats. Typically, a trip from Bulls Bridge to Braunston was completed in two working days. Their rapid progress was further aided by the deeper channel and by the comparatively finer lines with which the craft were constructed. It is easier now to put in a bigger engine and to shape the boat more crudely. A team spirit prevailed so that everything was organised with precision and meals were produced just when a flight of locks had finished and the hungry crew was free. Tea was consumed between locks and copious amounts of it were drunk. This habit had developed from carrying vast quantities of tea to Birmingham, condensed milk to Tring, as well as sugar, plenty of coal for boiling the kettle, which stood sentinel on the range, and there were no water rates at the tap. Boatwomen aficionados would make sure that the water cans were filled at the tap that produced the best brew. Washing was not done on Mondays, but when the opportunity arose during long, lock-free sections.

Working a pair of boats through a lock on the GU used to take about three and a half minutes. A lot of people today take fifteen. It was easier in those days because almost every lock had gate paddles (without baffles) and ground paddles. When leaving a lock, the gates were left open. Ideally, a crew of three was needed to work a pair with optimum efficiency.

A boatwoman sits on the cross bed while drinking tea on the folded-down table. The modesty flap on the right divides the cross-bed from the side-bench. (Hugh McKnight Photography)

Above: Coal pours into the hold of *Cypress*. The conveyor is fixed but the boat is moved to ensure a balanced load. (Tom Chaplin)
Below: Once fully loaded, the top planks are put in place and the side cloths pulled up and tied. (Tom Chaplin)

Above: Then top cloths are positioned over the planks and side cloths. (Tom Chaplin)
Below: Before setting off the boat is scrubbed to remove the coal dust. (Tom Chaplin)

The lock gates are being opened using the boatman's rope trick. (Tom Chaplin)

Great skill was needed for one person to take two loaded boats through Winkwell while the other member of the crew opened the swing bridge. *Bletchley* and *Bedworth* are a pair of large Woolwich Town Class boats built for the GUCCCo in the 1930s. This photo, taken in 1968, shows the pair working for Willow Wren while still in BW colours. (Tom Chaplin)

The state of the locks ahead would be known as oncoming craft would indicate how many locks were in their favour. Entering the lock, the two crew on the boats would shut their respective gates, while at the same time the lock wheeler would open all the paddles and the water flow would help to slam the gates shut. If the boat was going uphill, the motor would push the gates open. If downhill, a rope from the mast with a slipknot round the gate handrail would pull the gates open as the boat was brought astern. The rope would release itself as the boat came out of the lock.

Probably what was most striking for somebody brought up on the land was the family cohesion on the boats. Many readers will have grown up with parents whose jobs took them away from home during working hours while the children attended school. For boat people,

With decked-over tank holds, Clayton's *Tay* and *Leam* return from Banbury to collect another load of tar at Leamington Gas Works. The pair are being worked single-handed down the Napton flight. (Tom Chaplin)

home and work had no clearly defined boundaries; for many there was no school and life had to be lived in a very confined space.

The cabin was very well laid out: a double bunk folded out across the boat at the rear of the cabin while in the centre, a cupboard door dropped down to form a table. By the entrance was the coal range for heating and cooking, while the coal box also served as a step from which to climb out to the cockpit. The cabin was grained (painted so as to look like wood) and was finished off with curtains in front of the bunk and a carpet or rug on the floor. Lace-edged plates were hung on all available vertical surfaces and the decoration was finished off with crochet work, brass knobs and brass rails. A swivelling oil lamp provided a cosy glow. Even the Duke of Kent, when he opened the newly widened section of the GU in 1934, proclaimed the narrow boat cabin 'a very cosy place'.

Cabins had to conform to a standard laid down by the Canal Boat Acts of 1877 and 1884. Back in the nineteenth century, a key reformer was George Smith of Coalville. He had succeeded in improving the conditions of women and children in the brick-making industry before turning his attention to the plight of the boat families. They appeared to him in two polarised forms: the sinful who lived in squalid conditions, and a pious minority of owner-boatmen who refused to work on a Sunday and lived aboard immaculate craft. The result was

Mrs Humphries in 1965, surrounded by lace-edged plates amid the splendour of her boat cabin. (Hugh McKnight Photography)

Salt destined for Weston Point being loaded by hand into *Argo*. Just above the first 'C' can be seen the registration number of the boat, believed to be the last boat registered. (Tom Chaplin)

This 1959 photo shows Willow Wren Canal Carrying Co.'s Braunston yard, by the bottom lock. The inside boat, *Kingfisher*, has a bow cabin. The cruiser is *Willow Wren*, owned by Captain Vivian Buckley-Johnson, a merchant banker who bankrolled the company, which was founded in 1953. (Tom Chaplin)

The Salvation Army's boat *Salvo* moored at Braunston. Barlow's boats were built beneath the rusty roof behind, while the asbestos-roofed building was the engine shop and fuel store. (Tom Chaplin)

the Report of the Committee of Enquiry into the Practice of Living-in on Canal Boats 1920–21 and the Canal Boat Acts. The latter specified the minimum volume of cabin per person, and a boat would be registered with local authorities for specific numbers of adults and children.

Working boats still denote their place of registration and number on the side. Those built in Braunston were usually registered at Daventry; FMC iron boats at Birmingham. Probably the last boat to be registered was Anderton Canal Carrying Company's *Argo*, which it purchased in 1968. Craft would be periodically examined and the size of the crew checked so there are many tales of children being sent off to join sympathetic crews elsewhere when the inspector was expected. Several horse boats were built with bow cabins to give extra accommodation for children, one of the last of which to trade was Willow Wren's *Kingfisher*. The system became easier to manage after motors were established and large families were able to work a pair of boats.

Overcrowding was always a problem but there were various ways of alleviating their difficulties. Because it was a tight-knit community, often the eldest children would go to live with grandparents, uncles, aunts or even cousins. Another system was to take on a second pair of boats with the same company and the family would work all four as an entity. The second pair would be run by teenagers while the first pair continued to handle the cooking and washing.

The boatpeople were not totally Godless. There were various chapels around the system. The Salvation Army had a pair of boats with a hold covered over which it used as a centre from which to help boatpeople with their problems: for example, writing letters and

The Revd Chapman visiting a boat family at Brentford. The motor is still in faded GU colours, while the butty is painted in a more elaborate BW style. (Tom Chaplin)

persuading them to drink tea and coffee rather than alcohol. They were usually stationed at Hawkesbury Junction, or Sutton Stop as it was known by the boatmen, where boats waited to pick up orders for loading coal.

Brentford was a celebrated gathering place for boats loading goods from barges that had come up the Thames from the London Docks. Here the London City Mission had a large house at the Butts where the Revd Chapman was pastor after the war. They provided Sunday schools, prayer meetings and welfare advice and assistance.

Alienated from the land by their nomadic lifestyle and the illiteracy it engendered, the community turned in on itself to produce its own unique culture and traditions.

Did you know?

Rose and Arthur Bray moved into their brand new butty *Raymond* in 1959. Rose was a very sociable person but no one ever saw her ashore during the rest of her working life. They retired when the last contract to the 'Jam 'Ole' (the jam works at Southall) ceased in 1970.

Boats often tied up together in the evening, either in locations where relatives or ex-boatman were living, or where they waited for orders or loading. It was difficult to entertain much in the small cabins so usually they met in canal-side pubs, most of which had stables. Often someone would play an accordion, there would be tap-dancing, songs and all the news of the cut. Best of all, it was customary at most of these establishments to charge the company for the stabling but provide the boatmen with a free pint.

Some claimed, however, that either you worked so hard that you didn't have time to drink or you didn't earn enough to survive, and certainly no one could afford to drink heavily every night. In latter years, going to the cinema became a popular pastime and some would aim to reach a specific location on a Saturday night for entertainment.

Boat children's education was necessarily spasmodic, relying on a few hours spent at a local school while the boats were tied up waiting to load. Legislation requiring records of attendance was difficult to enforce and unreliable. However, after the Second World War, improvised schools were set up at Bull's Bridge and Brentford depots and the Birmingham Education Authority set up a hostel where children could stay while attending the local school, but it was unpopular. The author knows of one boatman who escaped and worked his way down the canal until he found his parents. Another boat family could not cope with their young daughter living away from them so they moved to a house to enable their children to attend a local school.

These increasing levels of education widened horizons and, as standards of living on land improved, life afloat compared increasingly unfavourably. By the 1960s, working-class housing had improved dramatically with the assistance of rebuilding programmes or improvement grants. The boatman moving ashore could be offered a centrally heated council house or flat with an indoor toilet and bath, and, with factory wages, might even contemplate a washing machine on hire purchase. The future afloat was already insecure but the defection of the workforce to the land was the final thrust that trade could not survive.

Jack James, a former Number One (the name given to owner boatmen), dressed in traditional best costume. (Tom Chaplin)

The *Chiltern* heads north in thick fog. The steerer is unable to see the bow. Many boatmen moved at night without using a headlamp because they found that the light was merely reflected back by the mist. Because they knew the route well, they could identify the outline of bridges without lights. (Tom Chaplin)

4
Traditional Painting

Perhaps the best-known aspect of narrow boat painting is roses and castles, probably because it is an art form found only on these craft. However, a close examination of a traditionally painted boat will reveal that in practice they were often only a small part of the overall painting scheme and on the GU fleet, could be very insignificant.

It is difficult to know when traditional painting on narrow boats began. There are a few early prints but they usually feature Pickford's boats, on which the painting was limited to a diamond motif. Photographs indicate that in the late nineteenth century, the major carriers used a black and white colour scheme with the company's name appearing in large letters. Whether this was to comply with the regulation that the owner's name must be clearly shown or whether it developed as early advertising is not clear. As time passed, distinctive colour schemes gradually emerged; for example, FMC adopted green and red in 1921. In fact, by the 1950s, black and white was virtually obsolete. Typically, a narrow boat would have cabin sides with rectangular panels and large lettering – often with the carrier's name painted in an arc that occupied the whole space of the panel. Any gaps would be filled with either scrolls or roses and most butties had a castle panel as well.

A traditional cabin side reflected nineteenth-century tastes: large, deeply shadowed lettering, akin to that found on fairgrounds and such like; roses and castles similar to illustrations found on papier-mâché trays and clock dials; and scrolls resembling those on wagons of the period. Many of the boats were sign-written by boatyard painters rather than

Black and white Anderton boats wait at Runcorn in 1900. (Hugh McKnight Photography)

A fleet of BW boats at Brentford waiting to load. At the beginning of nationalisation, the boats were painted with quite a lot of detailing. The motor with two children is still in FMC colours. (Tom Chaplin)

The well-painted and distinctive colour scheme of the Anderton Canal Carrying Co. The *Shad* shows how effective scrolls could be. (Tom Chaplin)

sign-writers. This became evident when this author tried to get a boat traditionally painted and showed a professional sign-writer some photographs. He said he could not do it because it was 'wrong'. Close scrutiny reveals that quite often the shading on the lettering on the cabin sides was in the opposite direction to the shading on the boat's name.

Another important element in the painting of the boat was the addition of diamonds or lozenges on the side, with an extra fine line added between colours. Red and green were contrasted with white or yellow in a harlequin pattern. Narrow boat cabins and stern doors were routinely grained throughout – a practice also widespread in Victorian houses. On Samuel Barlow boats, water-based paint was common. It dried much more quickly than oil-based paint, enabling the completion of an entire cabin in a day. Sometimes it was done merely for an overall impact but occasionally it was so meticulously rendered that it could be mistaken for real wood. The author was once completely fooled by a steel diesel tank with an abundance of knots. Once the cabins were grained, roses, castles and geometrical designs would be added to the panels. A cabin could have up to ten castles.

The styles varied according to the boatyard and the individual artist. Most painters started as apprentices, initially grinding and mixing the paint and later being entrusted with the background colours. The apprentice imbibed his techniques from the master. Stylistically, there was a North/South divide. Roses from the Trent & Mersey Canal, known as 'knobsticks', were much more realistic than the stylised ones from the South.

The *Stour*, moored at Clayton's wharf at Oldbury at the very end of their carrying in 1966. The site is now under the M5 motorway and all the gasworks have gone. The photo shows the Clayton style of roses painted by Fred Winnet and the lettering expanded out to fill the main panel. (Tom Chaplin)

Willow Wren's *Grebe*, ex-FMC *Antelope*, undergoing a repaint in the dry dock beside Braunston Bottom Lock. The cream on the doors and on the cabin interior is the base for graining. (Tom Chaplin)

Today's roses tend to be white, red and yellow with the addition of a few small daisies, whereas in the past, pink was quite frequently used as a fourth colour and a miscellany of other flowers, even rosebuds, completely filled the space with an exuberant bouquet. Essentially, the art has been pared down to represent only a small part of what was originally the norm.

There were also various geometrical designs and many boatyards developed their own distinctive motif. Especially outstanding were the Number Ones who went to greater extremes to have beautiful homes, usually sporting two castle panels on each side of the boat, which was often replete with lozenges. Some companies, such as Samuel Barlow, always had well-painted boats with varying amounts of adornment on each. FMC strove to be equitable with a fairly basic colour scheme, which aimed to have the boats virtually identically painted so that the crew couldn't make unfavourable comparisons with each other's craft.

In the 1930s, the GUCCCo built its large fleet of boats. Keen to project an image of modernity, it tried to simplify the painting and had the company name painted in a straight line, keeping roses and castles to a minimum. When the war came, their livery became still starker, retaining only the company's initials on the side.

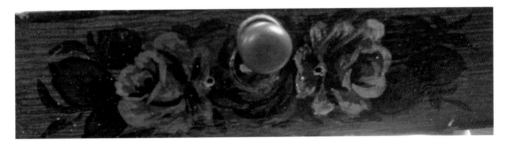

Knobstick roses on a crumb drawer. (Tom Chaplin)

This horse bowl by Jones of Leighton Buzzard shows not merely roses and daisies, but a wide variety of flowers. His trademark cream motif decorates the red base. (Tom Chaplin)

Ron Hough was the last of the professional painters who had served an apprenticeship at a narrow boat building yard. Here Ron adds rosebuds. (Tom Chaplin)

With nationalisation, the GU fleet, and a year later, the FMC fleet, became part of BW. At that time, the new BW, which was a division of the Docks & Inland Waterways Executive, was run by demobbed army officers and it is said that the new blue and yellow livery was the brainchild of an officer whose regimental colours they were. Although both colours had been used on a variety of boats before, blue had never been dominant in any large fleet. To start with some detailing persisted, and sometimes there were even a few additional colours, but BW was keen to abolish the roses and castles. This provoked a national protest, led by the Inland Waterways Association (IWA) that had been formed in 1946, with the result that BW's resistance was conquered and roses and castles reinstated.

Left: Jess Owen worked for Charity Dock at Bedworth until after the end of long-distance boating. (Tom Chaplin)
Below: George Baxter painted for S. E. Barlow at Tamworth. (Tom Chaplin)

Joe Skinner was the last of the Number Ones. He worked the boat with his wife Rose until 1959, shortly after their mule, Dolly, slipped into the canal and died of pneumonia. The painting, carried out in 1956 by Herbert Tooley of Banbury eight years before this photograph was taken, is typical of a Number One, with two castles on the side and fancy graining. (Tom Chaplin)

A castle from Lee Atkins' yard at Polesworth. (Tom Chaplin)

A castle painted by Frank Nurser in 1951. (Tom Chaplin)

Above left: A castle painted by Jess Owen of Charity Dock, Bedworth. (Tom Chaplin)
Above right: A cabin table by Harry Fenimore, painter at Bushell Brothers of Tring. (Tom Chaplin)

This 1959 photo, taken one evening at Hawkesbury Junction, shows Barlow's *Lucy* at her best, not only in the exuberance of the painting but in the graceful shape of her hull. (Tom Chaplin)

This time they cheated and had transfers made using artwork produced by Frank Jones of Leighton Buzzard, who was a favourite painter. How much time this actually saved was debatable because a skilled boatyard artist could paint very quickly, especially if he was doing several together. As one painter said, it would have taken him longer to go to the store, collect the transfers, sign for them, get back to the boat, cut them, soak them and fix them, than it would simply to paint them. Had a representative watched both operations, perhaps a different conclusion would have been reached. As a further irritant, the uniform size did not always adequately fill the varying spaces on individual craft. It was a poor start to a working relationship between employer and boatmen, signalling as it did a predilection for decisions made from a desk rather than from observation.

Until then there had been scope for idiosyncrasies such as a dog or Players' Hero. The transfers brought distinctiveness to an end and North and South were no longer

Right: Bulls Bridge Depot lay-by. Boats waited here to receive orders to load at either Brentford or Regents Canal Dock. The lay-by was virtually opposite the junction that gave access to the dock. (Tom Chaplin)
Below: The castle on the left is a Jones painted transfer: on the right is an original, painted in 1950 and showing considerably more detail. (Tom Chaplin)

On the GU in 1962, the small Woolwich, *Comet*, displays the new austere painting and is paired with a River Class butty. (Tom Chaplin)

distinguishable. By 1960, the overall scheme had been pared down still further. In 1962, as an economy, the graining inside the cabin was changed to cream alone and yellow was omitted entirely from the exterior. The once vibrant narrow boat had been relegated to a blue monochrome with yellow lettering. Even after privatisation, some boats stayed in their Cinderella livery but others were repainted and maintained in all their glory until the end.

Today, all sorts of ostensibly traditionally painted articles are available but a working boat was restricted to a few functional possessions. In prime position were the water cans, which sat beside the chimney. Then there was the dipper – a metal bowl with a handle – that functioned as a portable sink and was used for washing up, personal washing, shaving and preparing vegetables. Most boats also had a stool along with a coal box. The other two favourites were a galvanised bucket and a nose tin for the horse.

Measham teapots, known as 'barge wear', were used by some boatpeople but only rarely. Boatmen sometimes bought them as wedding or 'thank you' presents. They were sold at Measham at the top end of the Ashby Canal where coal was loaded. One old boatman recalled buying a teapot as a gift for someone who had helped his family when their boat was frozen in for a long time.

Finally, narrow boats externally had quite a lot of brasswork. Chimneys traditionally had three brass rings at the top but the author has never seen red painted between, as has become common in recent years. The chimney would have had either a brass safety chain or, after the Second World War, a chain made of brass gasmask clips. Sometimes the corner of the cabin would have a brass plate to protect the paintwork where people jumped on and off and these were always highly polished. The array of chimney brass and the water can arrangement were usually set off with a long-handled mop, brightly coloured and painted in spirals like a barber's pole.

Right: The chimney of *Shad* is decorated with three brass rings and a safety chain made from gasmask clips. The can is in the usual place, with the mop shaft passing through its handle to reduce the risk of losing it overboard if it were knocked by overhanging branches. (Tom Chaplin)

Below: *Crater* in 1964 was probably the last butty to support the tradition of attaching a horse's tail to the rudder. (Tom Chaplin)

Sometimes horse brasses were hung up in the cabin or attached to the brass chain for the chimney. This became more popular when boatmen had replaced their horses with diesel engines. A further relic of those days was a horse's tail that was sometimes hung from the rudder stock of a butty. The motor stern had several fenders arranged so that they sloped up slightly whereas today most people have ones that sag. They were always kept well scrubbed.

It was important to a boatman that the bows of his boat were always well-kept as it was the first thing that an approaching boater saw. The single navigation lamp, originally oil and often highly decorated, was positioned forward of the cratch. This triangular-shaped vertical board placed at the front of the hold to prevent water getting into the cargo was nicely painted by some companies, such as Blue Line and Samuel Barlow, but most merely covered it with canvas or tarpaulin. However, the boatmen brightened this up with white scrubbed ropework and often added a scrubbed fireman's hose across the top, which contrasted well with the tarpaulin. This, together with clean paintwork, could smarten up the dullest boat. Other adornments were cabin blocks, where the top plank running over the hold rested on a block of wood sitting on the cabin top, which was painted with roses or castles, while motor boats often had what is termed a pigeon box, designed to let light and air into the engine room.

Any description of a traditional narrow boat is at risk of making the painting appear to have been more than a little haphazard and perhaps something of a hotchpotch. The reality was quite otherwise, for close scrutiny revealed that the omission of any part of the painting scheme would have destroyed the perfect harmony of the whole. It was truly a work of art.

Ian looks immaculate with scrubbed rope and paintwork having just loaded at Baddesley Colliery and waiting at Atherstone Top Lock for the butty *Iona* to work up the flight. (Tom Chaplin)

5
The Decline of Commercial Carrying

Although the death knell of canal transport was sounded by developments occurring after the Second World War, its readiness to sink under these pressures arose from longstanding problems: problems that had long been debated but largely ignored. It is widely believed that the railways were greatly responsible, but while they undoubtedly contributed, the situation was in reality far more complex. Relations between canal and railway companies varied enormously depending on circumstances, and occasionally they worked to the advantage of canal companies.

The canals reached their zenith during the Edwardian period. Typical of the expansion was the erection in 1875 of the Anderton Boatlift and the building of the Slough Arm of the GU in 1882.

Did you know?

The Birmingham & Warwick Junction Canal, constructed in 1844, served as a shortcut between what is now the underside of Spaghetti Junction and the GU at the bottom of Bordesley (Camp Hill) Locks. It was only 3 miles and six locks long. In 1926, it carried 413,504 tons, the equivalent of 16,540 loaded boats. Since most of the traffic tended to be one-way, this would indicate about 33,000 boat movements per year, or about one boat every five minutes during a ten-hour day.

While there have been numerous inquiries into the state of the canals, by far the most extensive was the 1906 Commission, which confirmed that in some cases railways were detrimental to canals. Despite this, it was only in 1963 that the canals and railways were fully separated with the formation of BW.

The system of tolls was complex. Acts of Parliament had set maximums for some classes of cargo; for example, road stone was free of tolls so that canal companies would not adversely affect road construction. Railway and Canal Acts in 1854 and 1888 attempted to prevent railway companies from charging inflated tolls.

In practice, for self-preservation, canal companies gave reduced rates when goods had to be competitive. Coal, having been carried up the Thames for Witney Blankets, had reduced rates on the Oxford Canal so that it could compete with coal from the Forest of Dean. Annual licensing was only introduced in 1963 when it was too late, and most of the commercial traffic had terminated.

Left: Anderton Boat Lift opened in 1875 linking the Trent & Mersey Canal with the River Weaver and, hence, Weston Point Docks. A pair of BW boats is moored 50 ft below. (Tom Chaplin)

Below: The Slough Arm was only built in 1882. The last load carried was probably in 1969 when steel piling was offloaded beside the River Colne aqueduct. The river below was being made navigable for gravel barges. The motor was *Chiltern*, one of a group of three motors that were the last wooden boats built by FMC at Uxbridge. (Tom Chaplin)

Steam-powered boats were usually prevented by the by-laws from operating on railway-owned canals, which objected to the erosion caused by their speed. This conforms to the classic image of railway ownership but transport logistics sometimes favoured a waterway element. The Birmingham Canal Navigations (BCN) were owned by the Midland Railway Company, which used them very successfully as feeders to its own system. In 1925, this traffic amounted to 4,362,348 tons (175,000 loaded boats), much of it between canal-side factories and railway interchange basins. Even in 1947, it was still as much as a quarter of a million tons.

Similarly, when the Shropshire Union Railway & Canal Carrying Company gave up its large fleet of boats in 1921, a group of industrialists in the Black Country formed the Midland & Coast Carrying Company to create competition with railways. Nevertheless, there were casualties, such as the Uttoxeter Canal, where the canal bed was converted to a railway track.

The railways were superb for moving large loads but the narrow boat's smaller capacity sometimes better fitted the customer's needs. A local coal merchant with a wharf could have 25 tons at a time delivered from different collieries supplying various grades of coal and then distribute by horse and cart. The railways could offer only trainloads of the same type of coal and it had to be unloaded promptly.

Through most of their commercial life, canals gained in efficiency. Those such as the northern section of the Oxford Canal and the BCN were straightened and improved and, from 1912, the introduction of diesel motor boats further increased speed.

In 1935, the newly formed GUCCCo embarked on a massive expansion programme and built 373 craft. Many of the steel Star and Town Class boats are still around today. Already there were signs of the problems to come because it had difficulty finding enough crews and many of the boats actually remained idle. They also built warehouses and improved handling

Ara and *Archimedes* in the twenty-first century, delivering pre-packed fuel, diesel and calor gas while ice-breaking in Little Venice. Both boats were built as Harland & Wolff Star Class during the 1930s. (Tom Chaplin)

facilities. The decline in narrow boat carrying was therefore by no means consistent and while it was reduced overall, in some areas trade continued to flourish.

Well into the twentieth century, it was generally considered viable. Ovaltine built a new works beside the GU at Kings Langley and commissioned a fleet of narrow boats for carrying coal to their works. With Regents Canal Dock incorporated into the GU, companies like Heinz and Lyons built factories powered partly by coal from canal-side collieries in the Midlands and designed to use canal-borne imported ingredients. Between the wars, there was a large growth in gas and electrical industries and many of these, too, were built to take advantage of the waterways. George Cadbury observed that, 'Inside London, the old Regents Canal is so lined with wharfs, warehouses and factories that it has the appearance rather of an extended dock than a waterway for through traffic.' The GU owned considerable land in the Birmingham area and to promote freight, any company renting a wharf was entitled to a rent reduction in proportion to the tonnage carried there by canal. This encouraged quite a few timber merchants because imported wood could be stored cheaply while seasoning.

When in 1947 the government nationalised the railways, it found itself compelled to take over all of the railway-owned canals and those it had controlled during the war, in addition to their associated carrying companies. IWA was a strong lobby fighting to keep many waterways open. Sometimes it prevented closure by securing a carrying contract: Parliament could only extinguish a right of navigation if it could be shown that the waterway in question had ceased to fulfil its intended purpose.

A notorious case was the carrier John Gould of Newbury, who bought a pair of narrow boats in 1949 from Harvey Taylor of Aylesbury and obtained a contract to move top soil from Newbury to Hampton for T. Harrison Chaplin Ltd. Aware that the Kennet & Avon was on the government's hit-list, he signed a long-term agreement, but a couple of months later the canal was closed for an indefinite period for safety reasons. John successfully took the Docks & Inland Waterways Executive (which became BW) to court and prevented the government from passing a bill to close the canal. By then, public opinion and the efforts of volunteers combined to save the canal, which has since been fully restored.

In 1953 the British Transport Commission (BTC) set up a survey, chaired by Lord Rusholme. Although he favoured the development of the larger waterways such as the Aire & Calder, he recommended closing many narrow canals, including the Kennet & Avon and Southern Oxford. The uncertainty discouraged investment and helped to generate statistics of decline, which in turn were used to justify their neglect. In 1963, Charles Hadfield, the canal historian, found that 'only one other man on the Board knew anything about canals and he had been chairman of the Inland Waterways Redevelopment Committee and was only knowledgeable about canals they were thinking of closing. He didn't know anything about those that were open'.

With a door-to-door flexibility that neither the railways nor canals could match, lorries were increasingly able to undercut both, especially for the short-haul jobs required by some of the new light industries. Canal-side factories were no longer built and many collieries became worked out. In 1949, 143,000 tons of gasworks by-products were carried on the BCN but the closure of gasworks because of North Sea gas resulted in Clayton ceasing to carry. Today, a business park and housing development stand on the site at Croxley formerly used by stationery makers John Dickinson, once the largest consumer of coal on the GU. This is a pattern echoed throughout the country.

Above: Alongside Tom Rolt's *Cressy* is John Gould's *Colin*, moored for the night at Sonning on her way back to Newbury in 1950. Splendid graining is evident between the two panels. The white panel with the boat's name is in classic Bushell Brothers style. (Tom Chaplin)

Right: The notice that heralded the intended closure of the Kennet & Avon. (Tom Chaplin)

DOCKS AND INLAND WATERWAYS EXECUTIVE
SOUTH-WESTERN DIVISION

KENNET & AVON CANAL

Owing to the condition of Heales and other Locks, the Navigation will be closed from upstream of Heales Lock No. 93, 13 miles, 50 chains from Reading, to downstream of Burghfield Lock No. 103, 5 miles, 5 chains from Reading, until further notice.

BY ORDER
A. C. LISLE
Divisional Waterways Officer

Dock Office, Gloucester.
31 May, 1950

Willow Wren boats waiting to unload coal at Croxley Mill near Watford. At one time, barges also brought up raw materials for papermaking, while narrow boats took away the finished product. (Tom Chaplin)

Changes in industrial processes also eliminated the need for canal transport. Typical is the pottery industry, where for 200 years china clay was dried and shipped around the coast from Cornwall to Chester, Runcorn, Ellesmere Port, etc., and carried by narrow boat to the factories. The little that remains is now transported in slurry form in tankers and most production has moved to China.

South-bound coal traffic had also been slowed down by one particular pound at Atherstone, into which a red sludge was discharged from a road stone quarry, quite legally, and in return for payment. The silting-up that ensued made this stretch a nightmare for commercial traffic and by the end of the 1960s even the much lighter, lower-draught pleasure boats were having difficulty passing. It undoubtedly helped to crystallise the growing conviction among traders that the BTC and then BW wished to divest itself of the need to maintain canals to a commercial standard.

Over the years, many sacked and bagged cargoes succumbed to palletisation and forklift trucks, which were incompatible with narrow boats. While the nation moved on, narrow boats continued to depend on the shovel and the wheelbarrow. A boatman recalled that in the 1950s, 'In the whole of the five towns [Potteries], there was not a single mechanical grab for unloading boats'. Even the waterside warehousing service that had made a major contribution no longer fitted in with modern accounting systems, frowning as they do on 'dead' money tied up in stock piles, or for that matter, in slow transit.

In 1951, the National Coal Board had imposed loading charges for canal-borne coal, ostensibly to cover extra handling costs, but doubts arose when loading gear at some of the collieries was destroyed or closed around the same time. While individual collieries may have attempted such a step previously, nationalisation meant a totally co-ordinated move. The IWA declared that, 'On all sides there seems evidence of a quite deliberate intention to put an end to the canals.'

Although the GU had increased the use of Regents Canal Dock, strong restrictive practices from militants created delays and removed the competitive edge that canals had enjoyed through rapid over-side loading from ships. A boatman in the early 1960s described how a 'pocket handkerchief-sized tarpaulin' over the top of his load of timber could only be removed by a lighterman. Contravening this to avoid an overnight delay would have caused the company, Willow Wren, to be blacked.

Above: Narrow boats felt very small and vulnerable in the docks and the unions stopped the boatpeople from having control over how the cargo was loaded. (Tom Chaplin)

Below: In the late 1950s, BW replaced some of its ageing wooden boats with new River Class butties. The boatmen hated them because they did not steer well with a rounded stern. They also had a swim bow, which did not plough a channel well through mud and their fixed hatch covers meant that when empty, they were difficult to handle in a side-wind. None were transferred to Willow Wren in 1963. (Tom Chaplin)

Following the bad winter of 1962/63, BW decided to give up its carrying fleet. The largest private company, Willow Wren, reformed as Willow Wren Canal Transport Services Ltd and hired most of the BW fleet along with their captains. The new system of annual licensing was operative and the boatmen became self-employed. Yet despite the canals being frozen over from Christmas until March, virtually no contracts were lost.

With no coal needed from the Midlands southwards and nothing coming up from the docks to Brentford, the end was inevitable. Yet, surprisingly, optimism still prevailed: warehouses were built at Brentford and several new carrying companies appeared. In 1964, the newly formed Seymour-Roseblade obtained a contract to carry timber from Boston, Wisbech and Manchester into Leicester. This commercial traffic passing over the Foxton Summit helped to remove the threat of closure. In 1965, the Birmingham & Midland Canal Carrying Company was formed, largely with the capital of canal enthusiasts.

One of the last north-bound regular contracts from London was the carriage of grain to the Weetabix factory in Wellingborough. It was barged from the London Docks to Brentford, where it was transferred to narrow boats and brought up the GU and then along the Nene. In 1969, a new grain terminal was opened at Tilbury, downstream of London, which made the combined transport uneconomic. Today, Weetabix advertises that all of its grain is locally grown, so that contract would have ceased anyway.

The next year brought the end of the last three remaining coal runs and a change in the process ended the carriage of coal dust to the sewage works at Maple Cross, where it had been burnt with sludge. Croxley no longer needed coal, while the jam works at Southall, known as the 'Jam 'Ole', received a sizable grant to relocate to an area of heavy unemployment.

Meanwhile, in the North West, the two staple traffics were also lost. Feldspar to Dalby's for china-making ceased when the company went into receivership, and Seddon's saltworks no longer required coal after the company was taken over and modernised.

The final blow to trade was the growth in lorry transport and the building of motorways. Not only was there no way of improving the efficiency of the boats, but also standards

This Brentford facility with overhead cranes was opened in the late 1950s. In the foreground is a typical barge, which was loaded in the docks and towed up to Brentford ready for transhipment to narrow boat or into the warehouse. This 1965 picture shows *Coleshill* and *Cygnus* in Willow Wren Canal Transport Services colours, while the other pair is still in the former BW livery. (Tom Chaplin)

Above: Seymour-Roseblade's *Neptune* and *Cedar* in Leicester with a load of timber from Manchester in 1965. The captain, Jack Monk, was a descendant of Thomas Monk, the first builder of long-distance narrow boats. (Tom Chaplin)

Below: Grain being grabbed out of a barge and dropped into a narrow boat at Brentford in 1965. Although the grain was carried to Wellingborough for Whitworth Bros, it was said to be for the nearby Weetabix factory. In this photograph, Canadian grain had been brought by ship to London Docks, by barge to Brentford and by narrow boat to Wellingborough. (Tom Chaplin)

Above: This January 1969 view of Winkwell shows a pair of boats laden with grain and well sheeted-up. In the background are just a few cruisers where today there is a thriving boatyard and mooring basin. (Tom Chaplin)
Below: Loaded Willow Wren boats waiting to unload at Wellingborough on the River Nene, known to the boatmen as the Wellingborough River. (Tom Chaplin)

Above left: The sun sets on a cold winter's night in 1969 behind the unloading gear at Croxley. (Tom Chaplin)

Above right: A pair of new Admiral Class narrow boats loaded with coal and about to be unloaded by hand at Seddon's Salt Works, Middlewich in 1961. The holds are protected with hoops and canvas. (Tom Chaplin)

Below: This photograph of the 'Jam 'Ole' in Southall sums up the changes in industry that affected canal carrying. The colliery supplying the coal has closed, and neither the fruit pulp nor the piles of timber in the background – Great Western's railway sleepers – come to London Docks, which closed. Creosote was brought by water to treat the sleepers but natural gas rendered the gasworks obsolete and concrete sleepers are now used. With the aid of a government grant, the factory itself transferred to the North East. (Tom Chaplin)

Above: Unloading salt directly into a ship in Weston Point Docks, which saved wharfage charges. (Tom Chaplin)

Below: *Mountbatten* heads back up the Weaver after unloading salt into a ship. The M56 – under construction in the background – was ultimately detrimental to canal traffic. (Tom Chaplin)

of canal maintenance had declined, and the loss of depth caused by insufficient dredging meant smaller loads and slower journeys. But there was another reason: the shortage of boat crews, which was a considerable obstacle to maintaining contracts or obtaining new ones. Companies formed agreements not to poach each other's staff.

During the Second World War women had been recruited, some of whom wrote about their experiences. They concluded that the skills that formed part of the growing-up process of the true boatman/woman became second nature to them and could not simply be learned by newcomers, who never came near to matching the delivery times of traditional boat families.

Did you know?

Most boatmen and women could not swim and although they rarely fell into the canal, there were a few tragic accidents. Babies normally wore harnesses and reins, which were attached to the cabin top. They quickly learnt not to throw their toys overboard.

The workforce was the lifeblood of the narrow boat industry and its defection to the land was the final blow from which trade was bound to die.

Do commercial boats have a future?

Now that the motorways are no longer regarded as the panacea that they first appeared and air pollution and congestion in towns and cities has escalated, it is perhaps time to reconsider waterborne freight. Efforts to secure a more sustainable transport system have so far brought trams back to some areas, so why not water transport? Electrically powered swiftboats could take passengers and smaller goods into the heart of cities like Birmingham and Manchester.

Industry originally grew around the canal network, and instead of more housing development, consolidation centres and waste processing plants could again be built alongside waterways. For example, a warehouse adjacent to the BCN and close to the M5 could send retail goods into Birmingham city centre with distribution to shops undertaken by small electric vehicles. The boats could return with waste from stores, offices and local restaurants. This would only work for a small proportion of our total freight but in the areas where it operated it would make a huge difference to air and noise pollution. Carbon emissions drop by 80 per cent when freight is transferred to water. Department of Transport statistics reveal that every lorry mile in a city centre creates £1.43 worth of damage to buildings, health, etc. Boats can undertake reliable deliveries: they are not held up by congestion and traffic lights and they can keep going in all but the most inclement weather. When a light fall of snow paralysed London Transport buses in 2009, traffic on the Paddington Arm continued as usual.

It has to be said that because canal-side development has resulted in the loss of most wharves, compromises would undoubtedly have to be made if we were to replace them. Traffic would be short-haul so day-time staffing would be perfectly feasible, although as with HGV drivers, extensive training would be needed.

Above: A pair delivering aggregates to West Drayton from Denham in 2005. This short-haul traffic took heavy lorries away from congested roads through Uxbridge and West Drayton. (Tom Chaplin)
Below: *Cygnus* and *Coleshill* were the first pair of boats to be painted in the new Willow Wren Canal Transport Services Ltd colours. They are seen here a month after they attended the re-opening of the Southern Stratford-upon-Avon Canal in 1964. (Tom Chaplin)

A narrow boat going down the Thames in 1870. (Tom Chaplin)

Freight on the canal keeps the channel clear for pleasure craft, and adds interest and excitement to the waterways, particularly in winter. We are unlikely to see the return of the traditional narrow boats of the past, but although the boats of the future could never match them aesthetically, their contribution to our inner-city wellbeing has never been more urgently needed.

6
What Now?

Further Reading

Various books have been published about narrow bats and the following could be helpful as references (some were published many years ago but they are readily available from online second-hand sources):

Blagrove, David, *Bread upon the Waters* (Harrow: The Belmont Press, 1995 (first published 1984)).
A humorous account of life aboard a pair of Willow Wren boats in the early 1960s.
Chaplin, Tom, *A Short History of the Narrow Boat* (Reading: Riparian Owner Service Ltd, 1999 (first published 1967)).
Written while narrow boats were still trading, this gives a well-illustrated, concise account of narrow boats, their construction and how they were run.
Chaplin, Tom, *Narrow Boats* (London: Whittet Books Ltd, 1989).
A more detailed and well-illustrated account of how the boats were built, painted and operated.
Foxon, Tom, *Following the Trade* (Harrow: The Belmont Press, 2010).
Brilliantly conveys life running a single motor during the 1950s.
Knill, John, *John Knills' Navy* (Bath: Sir John Knill, 1998).
John Knill ran a small fleet of boats in the 1950s. Here he offers a lively description of his carrying years together with an account of his early involvement with the IWA.
Lewery, A. J., *Narrow Boat Painting* (Newton Abbot: David & Charles, 1974)
Tony Lewery painted the last of the Anderton boats and here describes in detail the styles and techniques of the boat painter's craft.
McKnight, Hugh, *Canal and River Craft in Pictures* (Newton Abbot: David & Charles, 1969).
Roberts, Jack, *Shropshire Union Fly Boats* (Cheshire: Canal Bookshop, 2015).
Smith, Emma, *Maiden's Trip* (Worcester: M. & M. Baldwin, 1987 (first published 1948)).
Emma Smith manages to convey a sense of enjoyment that transcends the hardships of a volunteer's life afloat during the Second World War.
Wilkinson, Tim, *Hold on a Minute* (Harrow: The Belmont Press, 2001 (first published 1965)).
Recounts running a pair in the 1950s.
Woolfitt, Susan, *Idle Women* (Worcester: M & M. Baldwin, 1986 (first published 1947)).
This book offers a comprehensive overview of life afloat and the training of volunteer boatwomen.

Magazines

Narrow Boats
www.narrowboatmagazine.com
Published quarterly, this heritage magazine includes old photographs and historical information as well as a round-up of planned boat gatherings.

Waterways World
www.waterwaysworld.com/
A monthly magazine that sometimes includes historical articles and publishes details of up-coming rallies.

DVD/Video
Sight Seen Partnership & IA Recordings.
www.iarecordings.org
A range of DVDs showing re-enactments of historic trips and skills.

Web Resources
www.canalcuttings.co.uk
Lists sightings of historic narrow boats, details of up-coming gatherings and events.

www.canalrivertrust.org.uk
Accessible historical information on a wide variety of narrow boat-related topics.

Places to Visit
It has been estimated that there are only about 250 ex-working narrow boats left on the 3,000-mile waterway system, so a random towpath walk is unlikely to be rewarded by a sighting. More reliably, they can be seen all the year round at the three major museums run by the Canal & River Trust where the cabin interiors are also on display.

National Waterways Museum, South Pier Road, Ellesmere Port, Cheshire, CH65 4FW.
Here it is possible to board and enter the cabins. Upstairs, in one of the large buildings, is *Friendship*, the horse-drawn boat, which was owned by the Number One, Joe Skinner. There are also many artefacts on display.
Website: https://canalrivertrust.org.uk

Gloucester Waterways Museum, Llanthony Warehouse, The Docks, Gloucester GL1 2EH.
Normally has three narrow boats afloat, many photographs and a range of painted ware.
Website: www.gloucesterwaterwaysmuseum.org.uk/

Canal Museum, Stoke Bruerne, Bridge Road, Stoke Bruerne, Towcester, NN12 7SE.
Has a good mock-up of a cabin interior and usually a boat afloat. It would be wise to check the website before visiting.
Website: https://canalrivertrust.org.uk

London Canal Museum, 12–13 New Wharf Road, London, N1 9RT.
Set beside Battle Bridge Basin, near King's Cross, has a butty cabin, exhibitions relating to life on the canal, painting, etc.
Website: www.canalmuseum.or.uk

Waterways World's Crick Boat Show, which takes place over the Spring Bank Holiday, always has some historic boats.

Braunston Historic Narrow Boat Rally generally attracts eighty to 100 working boats and it is usually held on the fourth weekend in June.
Website: www.braunstonmarina.co.uk/Events

Getting Involved
Friends of *President*
www.bclm.co.uk/support/friends-of-president-steam-narrowboat/205.htm
The restored steam narrow boat *President* belongs to the Black Country Living Museum and tours the canal system with butty *Kildare*. Friends help to maintain and crew the boats.

Historic Narrow Boat Club
Website: hnbc.org.uk
A pressure group that aims to preserve the heritage value of canals and working boats. They hold boat gatherings in various locations throughout the year.

Inland Waterways Association
Website: www.waterways.org.uk
Aims to protect and restore the waterways network and undertakes local and national campaigns.

The Narrow Boat Trust Co. Ltd
Website: www.narrowboattrust.org.uk
Offers hands-on experience for owners and novices alike aboard the pair *Nuneaton* and *Brighton*.